Original title:
The Quest for Meaning: Still in Progress

Copyright © 2025 Creative Arts Management OÜ
All rights reserved.

Author: Aurora Sinclair
ISBN HARDBACK: 978-1-80566-244-0
ISBN PAPERBACK: 978-1-80566-539-7

Shadows of What Could Be

In the corner, shadows dance,
Twisting tales of lost romance.
We chase them with our silly feet,
Only to stumble on life's defeat.

A rubber chicken in the light,
Squeaks a tune with all its might.
We ponder deep on what could flair,
A punchline hiding everywhere.

With every laugh that spills and climbs,
We find the joy in silly rhymes.
The shadows laugh and roll away,
While we just grin at their display.

The Map That Never Ends

I opened up a folded sheet,
A treasure map, oh what a feat!
But every line just leads to snacks,
And chocolate paths, with no turning backs.

X marks the spot... but oh dear me,
It points to my own lost TV!
With every clue, I take a bite,
Outsmarted by my appetite.

The compass spins, it jokes and teases,
Not once it finds what truly pleases.
But donuts wait as I explore,
So who needs treasure? I'd rather score!

Reflections on a Moving Canvas

A mirror cracked, yet still it shows,
The silly faces, and funny pose.
In every glance, a comic spill,
Reflecting dreams that give a thrill.

Canvas bright with colors wide,
A painter laughs, and starts to glide.
Each brushstroke dances, winks with glee,
Creating worlds where all are free.

The palette spins in endless jest,
With every hue, life feels the best.
Our reflections paint the skies anew,
Each laugh a stroke, each joke a clue.

Unraveled Threads of Existence

A ball of yarn rolled down the street,
Its tangled clues beneath our feet.
We tug and pull to find the gold,
But end up with stories, new and bold.

Grandma's knitting, what a sight!
She drops a stitch but that's alright.
With every loop, she spins a yarn,
Of knights and dragons with no harm.

Our lives unwind like spools of thread,
Each knot a memory, laughter spread.
So here we sit with yarn in hand,
Crafting joy in each silly strand.

Illustrations of Wandering Souls

In a land where socks wander free,
They tell tales of their mystery.
What lies inside each tangled thread?
Perhaps a world where green has bled.

Chasing dreams like jellybeans,
While floated thoughts wear silly scenes.
Each twist and turn a comic grace,
In this wide, timeless, absurd space.

A map drawn on a napkin old,
Direction given by a cat so bold.
With every 'meow' a riddle to solve,
In laughter's light, the days evolve.

So grab a friend, let's toss the rules,
Dance like pancakes, let's be fools.
No need for answers, let's have fun,
In this cartoon race, we've already won!

Threads of Connection in the Void

In the void where silence reigns,
We knit our hopes with silly chains.
Spaghetti strings of random thought,
A tangled web where wisdom's caught.

Conversations with an empty chair,
Each punchline flies through midnight air.
Did you hear the one with the spoon?
It sings a tune to the lazy moon.

Juggling clouds and juggling dreams,
Bouncing ideas like rubber beams.
The universe winks, it must agree,
That life's a joke, just wait and see.

So let's embrace the cosmic jest,
In this chaos, we find our rest.
With laughs as stars in skies above,
We float like feathers, light as love.

Eclipsed by Questions

Why do ducks quack in a line?
Do they conduct, or just wine and dine?
The moon wears shades, looks quite cool,
While we play hopscotch in a rule-less school.

What if fish had dreams of flight?
Would they dance in the moon's delight?
Each answer leads to chaos, true,
But isn't that how fun breaks through?

They ponder puzzles on a board,
Like stargazers with a light accord.
But with each riddle comes a giggle,
As they tumble down the cosmic wiggle.

Let's raise our hands and ask away,
Like toddlers lost in the light of day.
With wisecracks shared and dreams a-fry,
We'll turn our woes into a pie!

Breathe in the Unknown

In a world where jellyfish play chess,
And pickle-flavored dreams coalesce.
We sip on tea brewed from our wishes,
And dance with thoughts that make us swishes.

A ticklish breeze whispers secrets low,
As our hearts sway to the rhythm's flow.
What's that? A cloud with feet that pranced?
Let's hop on it, perhaps we'll be tranced!

Breathing in the awkward pause,
As we tell tales without a cause.
Each mistake a badge, a badge to wear,
On this rollercoaster of fresh air.

So let's toast to the absurd they say,
To stumbling gracefully through the day.
With a wink and a nod, let laughter grow,
In this circus of life, we'll steal the show!

A Heartbeat Amongst the Chaos

In a world of jumbled socks,
I search in vain, avoiding clocks.
A dance with spills, my coffee's plight,
I laugh amidst the blurry night.

Chasing dreams like a runaway cat,
While life throws pies, oh imagine that!
With each surprise, a wink or two,
I juggle fears, and laugh off the blue.

Amidst the clutter, a smile peeks,
In cracked mirrors, it softly speaks,
What's lost in the noise, I still have fun,
In this circus act, I'm never done.

So raise a glass to life's odd ways,
To tangled paths and crooked delays.
For in this chaos, I find my grace,
Each heartbeat a dance in a jumbled space.

Through the Mist of Uncertainty

Woke up today with socks that clash,
In a world where quicksand is cash.
The breakfast toast sings a funny tune,
As I debate if it's night or noon.

The map is lost, but so am I,
Chasing rainbows that just wave bye-bye.
With each wrong turn, I find a clown,
Who tells me the secret is upside down.

Through foggy thoughts, I prance and sway,
Sometimes it's wise to lose my way.
With giggles and gaffes, I roam the streets,
As wisdom trips over its own two feet.

So here's to doubts that dance and tease,
To tangled dreams that never cease.
In the mist where I draw my breath,
I find my joy in what feels like death.

Beneath the Canopy of Doubt

Under this leafy doubt-filled tree,
I ponder life while sipping my tea.
The squirrels laugh at my puzzled brow,
As I play chess with fate, oh, what a row!

With each nut thrown, they scurry near,
I toss my worries, dissolve my fear.
The branches sway, what a funny sight,
As the clouds join in on my plight.

Growing wiser with every fall,
I chase the whispers of laughter's call.
For in this shade of what-ifs and maybes,
I find my strength in giggling babies.

So here's my toast to the path unsure,
To all the quirks that life can procure.
With a wink at the doubt that clings too tight,
I step out boldly into the night.

Songs of the Unsatisfied Soul

My heart strums tunes of missing keys,
As I search for meaning in the breeze.
Each note a hiccup, each chord a snicker,
While life plays hide and seek, oh what a kicker!

Dancing shadows sing out loud,
Of dreams that float beneath the cloud.
I'm just a jester with thoughts afire,
Chasing tilting thoughts like a frisky choir.

The unsatisfied soul, a capricious sprite,
Wanders in circles, yet feels so light.
With each misstep, I break into rhyme,
Making jokes of my doubting climb.

Pass the popcorn, I'm brewing cheer,
For every question that pricks my ear.
Through laughter's lens, I sketch the whole,
Transforming my fuss into a rollicking stroll.

Beneath the Surface of Existence

I found a sock beneath my bed,
It claimed to know where dreams are fed.
With a wink, it jumped to the floor,
"Life's a stage, go explore!"

In the fridge, a pickle wore a grin,
Said, "I'm brined but full of sin!"
I laughed and said, "What do you mean?"
"Just relish life, it's quite the scene!"

My cat's been reading ancient scrolls,
Prowling deep among the dolls.
He paused, then with a thoughtful meow,
"Answers are like hairball—just vow!"

And as I danced on tiptoe gleeful,
I tripped on thoughts that felt quite lethal.
Yet giggles bubbled from my core,
Because pondering's never a bore!

Navigating the Labyrinth of Self

I sailed a boat made of cereal,
Through a sea of thoughts, quite ethereal.
The marshmallow islands whispered, "Free!"
"Just don't mistake them for me!"

In the mirror, my reflection winked,
"It's hard to tell if I'm dead or linked!"
I grinned back, brushing my hair,
"It's all a puzzle, but who needs a spare?"

An old shoe spoke, wanted to chat,
"Life's too short to wear just that!"
I rolled my eyes and said with flair,
"Let's walk this maze without a care!"

So off I went with mismatched socks,
Tangled thoughts and paradox clocks.
Laughter echoed down the hall,
In this maze, I'm having a ball!

Colors of a Distant Horizon

I painted my hopes on a canvas wide,
With gummy bears as my guide.
They told me, "Pastels taste like the best!"
"Just don't let your dreams take a rest!"

A rainbow came out to play today,
Wore sunglasses to keep blues at bay.
"Why walk when you can slide?" it said,
"Let's color the sky instead of dread!"

A banana peel became my muse,
"Slip and slide, you've got nothing to lose!"
I laughed till I fell right off my throne,
Finding joy in hues that I'd never known.

The world's a palette, so bright and spry,
With every shade, we learn to fly.
So grab a brush and join the spree,
Let's paint our laughter, wild and free!

The Silence Between Questions

I asked my dog what life's about,
He rolled his eyes and started to pout.
"Just feed me treats and throw the ball,"
"The answers will come, just stall!"

A cactus claimed it had the key,
"But only if you water me!"
I chuckled softly, scratching my head,
"If only I knew why my hair's spread!"

In a cafe, ideas brewed strong,
Each sip of coffee felt like a song.
The barista smiled, said, "Sip slow,
Answers might come, but they're no show!"

Between sips of joy and bites of pie,
I pondered life's perplexing why.
Then glanced at the clock, oh so sly—
Elusive truths just waved goodbye!

Drifting Towards Understanding

On a boat made of thoughts, I sail,
With a map drawn in glitter, I fail.
The sea's full of waves, some funny, some wild,
I giggle at dolphins, so cheeky and styled.

Each island I see proves a whimsical tease,
Where the trees dance like socks in a breeze.
With a compass that points wherever it likes,
I chart my own course, dodging curious bikes.

The sun sets in colors that tickle my brain,
While clouds play hopscotch, forgetting the rain.
Each star is a giggle, a wink from above,
Navigating laughter is what I now love.

So here I drift, no clear end in sight,
With my boat full of snacks, everything feels right.
In this comic adventure, I'm free as a kite,
Chasing silly conclusions under moonlight.

Mosaic of Fleeting Insights

In a gallery filled with thoughts on the wall,
Each art piece whispers a riddle or call.
A banana in pajamas, a cat with a hat,
The meanings escape like a chirpy little brat.

I scribble my wonders on napkins and spoons,
Crafting deep wisdom from cartoons and tunes.
While jigsawing life with mismatched little pieces,
The humor in chaos, my laughter increases.

A toaster that dances, a fridge that can sing,
Each day adds a color, a twist in the fling.
I'm painting with giggles, my palette's a mess,
Finding joy in the puzzled, I feel so blessed.

In this whimsical world where insights are small,
I cherish the giggles and treasure them all.
For woven in jokes are the wisest of finds,
In the dance of the silly, true meaning unwinds.

The Unwritten Scroll of Life

With parchment so blank, I dabble in ink,
Each scribble a ponder, a laugh, or a wink.
An eyebrow raised high, a grin on my face,
As I write all my thoughts at a comic book pace.

The scroll rolls away, like a mischievous cat,
It flutters and giggles, where is it at?
I chase it in circles with glee and delight,
Down alleyways echoing laughter at night.

Each line that I pen holds a riddle or jest,
From unicorns prancing to pirates at rest.
And in every blank space that yearns to be filled,
Lies the humor of life, so joyfully thrilled.

This unwritten scroll, my daily delight,
Keeps me searching for laughter both day and night.
So bring on the quips, let the nonsense unfurl,
For I'm penning the stories of this wacky world.

A River of Questions Flowing

A river of queries flows through my mind,
Each ripple a giggle, so silly, so kind.
It babbles in rhymes, with splashes of cheer,
Where the fish are philosophers, wise yet austere.

Why do ducks wear suits, so twitchy and neat?
Is the grass truly greener, or just a deceit's?
The stones skip along, sharing secrets in jest,
While worms hold their meetings, debating the best.

Each twist of the river brings more joy to behold,
As the current of laughter, vibrant and bold.
I float on a leaf, enjoying the ride,
In this whimsical world, I take all in stride.

So I'll paddle my kayak through questions galore,
With a wink at the answers that swirl at the shore.
For in the funny flow of inquiry's stream,
I find the true meaning wrapped up in a dream.

Shadows of Tomorrow's Embrace

I chase my thoughts like runaway sheep,
They leap and prance, not a clue to keep.
With coffee in hand and socks that don't match,
I ponder life's riddles, but come up a scratch.

The moon winks at me as I trip on my shoes,
While pondering questions, I often confuse.
Is this a great journey, or just a tall tale?
As I dance with my doubts, I ponder and flail.

The cat thinks I'm silly, she's got it all right,
With naps and with purring, she conquers the night.
While I'm lost in the echoes of what might have been,
She dreams of catnip, a far better scene.

So here I sit laughing, at what life's become,
A circus of whimsies, a heart full of fun.
With shadows and laughter, I stride on ahead,
Chasing tomorrow while living instead.

A Horizon Beyond the Known

I peered at the sky, with a burger in hand,
Dreaming of futures both silly and grand.
With mustard and ketchup, I plotted my fate,
Then dropped my fries—oh, a twist of my plate!

The clouds formed a rabbit, or maybe a moose,
My friends all agreed, it's a metaphor loose.
"Let's toast to the chaos!" cried one with a grin,
While I searched for answers beneath all the din.

We wandered the streets, like lost overgrown kids,
In search of the meaning that our adulting hid.
With giggles and hiccups, we marched on our way,
While questioning life in a most humorous play.

So here's to the journey, the roads we will roam,
With snacks in our pockets, we'll still find our home.
An horizon of laughter, a canvas to paint,
We'll figure it out, even if it's quaint.

Wandering Through Uncertainty

I bought a new map, but it led me astray,
A zigzag of wonders that went the wrong way.
With snacks on my journey and tunes in my head,
I tripped over questions, my compass misled.

On corners of doubt, I stood still like a statue,
As pigeons debated my perplexing new tattoo.
"Just keep moving forward!" the wise seagull squawked,
While I laughed at the pathways that life had unlocked.

I asked a wise squirrel about wisdom and fate,
He just eyed my sandwich and said, "You can't wait!"
So I munched on my lunch, pondering all that—
Was it purpose I sought, or just crumbs for the cat?

In a world of confusion, I'm never alone,
With friends by my side, the seeds we have sown.
Uncertainty dances, with laughter as glue,
Together we wander—what else can we do?

Fragments of a Longing Heart

I gathered my dreams, but they slipped through my hands,
Like jelly on toast, or misplaced rubber bands.
With each fleeting daylight, I scribble and scratch,
While chasing my thoughts like a fast-moving hatch.

The echoes of wishes come back with a grin,
Reminding me gently where my heart has been.
With shoes that are squeaky, and mismatched old socks,
I ponder my choices while dodging the flocks.

A breeze whispers secrets from places unknown,
As I trip over memories like stones that I've thrown.
With laughter as armor, I'll plunge into night,
Digging for meaning in the glow of starlight.

So here's to the fragments that make up my core,
Each laugh and each stumble opens up a new door.
With a wink and a chuckle, I'll carry my art,
In the chaos of living, I treasure my heart.

Threads of Yearning in the Fabric of Time

Through tangled yarns we chase the sun,
Stitching laughter and the odd pun.
With needles wild, we mend our fate,
A patchwork quilt, we contemplate.

Each thread a giggle, a sigh, a dream,
In life's great fabric, we're never supreme.
My sweater's tight, like thoughts in my head,
But still, I wear it, and to bed I tread.

In pockets deep, I find lost toys,
Like hopes and wishes of girls and boys.
We twirl through fabric, whispers and threads,
Creating puzzles but making no beds.

As laughter echoes through spools of gray,
We twist and turn, in a fabric ballet.
So here's to the yarn, the knots, and the tugs,
A tapestry woven with love and with jugs.

Banners of Doubt in the Open Air

With banners waving, doubts take flight,
In the breeze, they dance, what a sight!
Should I wear stripes? Or should I go plaid?
Fashion choices can drive one quite mad.

A banner of skepticism flaps with flair,
While I question life through my messy hair.
Do ducks get sad when they can't find a pond?
Like all my musings, I just abscond.

The skies are vast, but my thoughts are not,
They twist and turn in a tangled knot.
Should I fly high, or stay on the ground?
My banners wave, though wisdom is drowned.

So let the doubts take their merry flight,
With giggles and chuckles, it feels so right.
In the circus of life, I'll wave them in cheer,
To doubts and banners, I lend an ear!

Secrets Woven in the Stars

Under starlit skies, we weave our tales,
With giggly secrets in cosmic gales.
Do stars get lonely, or just get confused?
When they blink, are they simply amused?

We count the dots, sip hot cocoa too,
A celestial map, but what's a clue?
If wishes can fly, where do they land?
In the heart of a friend, or a cat's furry hand?

The moon winks at us from high above,
Are those craters really from space love?
With each twinkle, a laugh spills out,
In a galaxy grand, we'll dance and shout.

So we write our secrets in stardust light,
With dreams that twinkle through the deep night.
Each shimmering wink, a riddled reply,
As we howl at the stars, oh me, oh my!

The Echo of an Undetermined Path

On paths unknown, we skip and sway,
Humming tunes in a backward way.
With every step, we search for fun,
But trips and falls, oh, those have begun!

Like echoes off walls, we bounce and roll,
With laughter weaving through each stroll.
If I take left, will I find ice cream?
Or just a tree that bursts with a scream?

Each footstep's a riddle, a hop of delight,
Balancing questions below the moonlight.
Is there wisdom in the muddy shoes?
Or just a puddle, with some colorful blues?

So here we wander, through paths undefined,
Collecting the echoes left behind.
With giggles unbridled, an unplanned map,
In this crazy maze, I'll take a nap!

Chasing Ghosts of Tomorrow

I chased a ghost down the hall,
It whispered secrets, made me fall.
I tripped on shoes from days gone by,
"Where's the party?" I did cry.

With every turn, a new surprise,
A piece of cake, a pair of pies.
The specter laughed, gave me a wink,
I chased my tail, forgot to think.

At lunchtime, ghosts made me a stew,
Tasted like socks, not like a brew.
They told me jokes, I rolled my eyes,
"To find tomorrow, eat some fries!"

So here I stand in biscuit dreams,
Chasing shadows, or so it seems.
A quest for snacks, both bold and strange,
Tomorrow's ghosts keep me deranged.

The Threads We Weave in Time

I grabbed a spool of colored thread,
To sew my dreams, I'll get ahead!
But tangled knots made quite a mess,
Now I'm a patchwork, I confess!

With every stitch, I made a joke,
My sewing machine began to smoke.
"Is this a dress or a multicolor wall?"
At least my cat thinks it's a ball!

In tangled yarn, I lost my way,
"We're going to Mars!" I heard them say.
But all we found was a lost sock,
Time travel's hard when it's a block!

Yet in the fibers, fun remains,
Laughter stitches through the pains.
In every loop, absurdity gleams,
We weave our hopes and stitch our dreams.

Explorations Beyond the Obvious

I took a step off beaten ground,
Where oddities and quirks abound.
The grass was pink, the sky was green,
I laughed so hard, could barely breathe!

I wore my hat upon my feet,
Found dancing ants that couldn't compete.
They marched in rows, they sang a tune,
Their band was led by a big raccoon!

Exploring realms where trees wear shoes,
I met a frog that loved to snooze.
"Hop on board!" he said with glee,
We sailed away on a cup of tea!

Yet still I ponder, as I roam,
If all this nonsense feels like home.
With laughter guiding every choice,
I'll follow whims and cheer with noise!

Reflections in the Glassy Void

I peered into a mirror wide,
Saw silly faces dancing inside.
"My bowtie's crooked, my hair's a fright!"
The glass just giggled, "You look alright!"

Each glance revealed a clown or two,
With rainbow wigs and flippers too.
"Join our circus, the show's about!"
I laughed so loud I nearly passed out!

Jumping through the frames of glass,
I bounced on hope, all I could amass.
The void said, "Why not take a chance?"
So I donned a tutu, lead the dance!

Reflections glinted with delight,
A world of laughter, pure and bright.
In every swirl, my doubts rescind,
In funny faces, joy begins!

Echoes of Unfinished Thoughts

I pondered on my breakfast toast,
While dreaming of a ghostly host.
What is life but crumbs and cheese?
I wonder if the cat agrees.

The sock drawer holds a mystic spell,
Its secrets bound, only it can tell.
Lost shoes and clothes that never fit,
Perhaps they're hiding, just for a bit.

The coffee spills, a darkened fate,
Would it brew a love or create hate?
The milk jug gurgles, who can say?
Is it a foe or a friend today?

Oh, laughter lingers in my mind,
In riddles and jokes, I seek to find.
A giggle echoes, a snicker too,
The meaning's hiding; maybe it's blue.

Paths Yet to Walk

I wandered down the sidewalk's edge,
Chasing thoughts like a silly pledge.
Each step a dance, each turn a grin,
Did I trip on purpose, or was that a win?

The map I drew leads nowhere fast,
With doodles that my buddy cast.
Twists and turns, where do they go?
A treasure hunt for lost bits of dough.

I pause to ponder, a squirrel stares,
Does he know why life seems unfair?
He gathers nuts, a wise little sage,
Is he planning for a nutty age?

In every step, the oddities glare,
I'm searching for wisdom, but it's a bear.
With giggles and mischief, I'll carry on,
On paths yet to walk, till the day is gone.

Whispers in the Void

In the silence, a whisper calls,
Perhaps it's me or a ghost in the walls?
What a hoot, this empty tone,
Is there wisdom in this far-off drone?

I shouted out for answers neat,
The echo laughed, then took a seat.
A riddle wrapped in giggles tight,
The void just grinned, under moonlight.

With every breath, my doubts take flight,
I ponder loudly into the night.
Do lost socks find their way back home?
The void just chuckles, "It's a roam!"

Amidst the silence, I search for truth,
But all I find is the joy of youth.
In whispers low, I tap my shoe,
The void reveals what's silly and true.

Searching for Fragments of Light

I peered into the fridge at night,
Searching for treasures, oh what a sight!
A pickle jar that's half-filled with hope,
Could it guide me? Maybe, just nope.

The flashlight flickers, a dance on the wall,
Is it here to help, or just to stall?
A dust bunny hops, and I must inquire,
Do you hold secrets, or just desire?

My dreams are scattered like crumbs on the floor,
I step lightly to avoid the lore.
In every shadow, I'm seeking a spark,
But all I find is a cackle in the dark.

Oh, fragments of light, where can you be?
Maybe I'll find you with my cup of tea.
In silliness, I'll chase away the night,
With laughter and love, until dawn's bright.

Symphonies of Unsung Stories

Once upon a Tuesday fog,
A cat played jazz on a log.
The fish all danced, the ducks wore hats,
While mice rolled by in purple spats.

Each note a tale, yet none they heard,
As squirrels hummed without a word.
A symphony of life so grand,
In the park where dreams are planned.

With every clap, the bushes sway,
A crazy tune of laughter's play.
Yet no one knows what song to sing,
In a world that's lost its spring.

So join the band, don't be shy!
Dance with leaves and touch the sky.
For even stories hide beneath,
The smiles we stitch with joyful wreaths.

Tracing Footprints on Sand

Tiny feet on sandy shores,
Chasing crabs and opening doors.
The tide rolls in with a silly grin,
While seagulls cheer the game we spin.

Tracing paths that never stay,
Footprints washed in the light of day.
One step forward, two steps back,
We dance our way through the whale's blue snack.

With buckets filled with hopes and dreams,
We sketch our plans with laughter's beams.
But waves arrive, as they always do,
To rewrite stories, fresh and new.

So let's make castles, tall and wide,
With seashells as our royal guide.
For in this game of ebb and flow,
We find the joy in tales we sow.

Tidal Waves of Thought

A thought waves crash like frothy seas,
So many ideas drift with the breeze.
One day it's a whale, the next a snack,
Swimming in circles, no turning back.

With each swell, my ponderings rise,
As jellyfish float, in endless disguise.
I ponder why my socks go missing,
In a tide that's always so dismissing.

Navigating through currents of doubt,
As sea turtles shout, 'Let's figure this out!'
A splash of humor, a dash of grace,
In the ocean of thought, we find our place.

So grab a surfboard, ride the fun,
Amidst our musings, we'll never be done.
For in every wave, a lesson awaits,
Crack a smile as curiosity creates.

Lanterns Upon a Shadowed Way

In pet shops bright, shadows mix,
As goldfish scheme their sly tricks.
Why did the cat steal the lamp?
To find the light for its next champ!

Lanterns flicker in nighttime's chase,
With fireflies leading a ball of grace.
Every glow a silly sight,
As we stumble home through the night.

With cautious steps, we tiptoe round,
While giggles leap from the underground.
Eccentric figures dance and twirl,
As lanterns sway with mischief's whirl.

So let the lights, though dim, ignite,
The laughter shared and dreams so bright.
For even shadows whisper cheer,
In this playful maze we hold so dear.

The Dance of Questions and Answers

In the ballroom of wonder, we twirl and spin,
Questions lead, while answers always grin.
Toe to toe, we stumble and sway,
What was the question? Oh, anyway!

With a hiccup here and a giggle there,
Dancing in circles, no sign of despair.
Each twirl uncovers a chuckle or two,
Is the meaning here? Maybe, maybe woo-hoo!

Under the disco ball of cosmic delight,
We giggle as truths hide, ready to fight.
Logic is tangled in vibrant attire,
Who knew confusion could light up a fire?

So we dance on the floor of delightful confound,
With each silly move, more joy is found.
As the evening wraps up and we take our seats,
Did we figure it out? Nah, but wasn't it sweet?

Footprints on the Sands of Search

Walking softly on grains of thought,
Every step takes me to places I sought.
I look for answers in the waves' little dance,
But they just laugh, say, 'Take a chance!'

Each footprint a puzzle, a riddle to crack,
Just when I'm close, the tide pulls me back.
A crab nearby shrugs, offers a grin,
'You're not the first to come looking for sin!'

Seagulls circle with wise little calls,
Yet my questions just bounce off their walls.
I wave at the shells, the old salty sage,
Who knows all the answers, but won't turn the page.

So I wander the beach, with my doubts in tow,
Chasing the sunset, where ideas can glow.
Every grain a reminder in this sandy quest,
It's not about answers; it's just about zest!

Hummingbirds in a Garden of Inquiry

In a garden where questions bloom like flowers,
Hummingbirds flit in their curious hours.
They sip nectar from mysteries sweet,
With every flutter, they dance and repeat.

'What's the buzz?' a bee jumps in the fray,
'Why do we bother?' it seems to say.
The flowers reply with a colorful sway,
'We bloom for the questions, and that's how we play!'

Pollinated thoughts in the sun's warm embrace,
The garden is lively, with no need for a race.
Dragonflies dart, perplexed by it all,
Cackling at answers that barely stand tall.

So let's gather the nectar from questions galore,
Each sip a delight, who could ask for more?
With hummingbirds leading, our spirals entwine,
In this garden of wonders, we're doing just fine!

Tides of Change in a Shallow Sea

The waves break softly, with flops and a splash,
They whisper secrets in a bubbly flash.
In this shallow sea, where thoughts like to play,
I'll find meaning maybe—just not today!

With every tide shift, the sand writes a tale,
Of fish chasing answers that always turn stale.
Crabs scuttle past, wise and quite sly,
'Is it deep or shallow?' they ask with a sigh.

The sun dips low, paints the foam with gold,
While jellyfish giggle, feeling quite bold.
In this watery world, where questions conjoin,
We find all the issues are simply a coin!

So I'll float on my raft of whimsical doubt,
Waves tickling my toes, nothing to shout.
For in this shallow sea, with laughter in tow,
Perhaps it's the journey and not where we go!

The Unfolding of Hidden Truths

I searched for wisdom in a shoe,
Yet all I found was a lost blue glue.
A sage once told me, 'Take a hike!'
But my GPS said, 'No, stay and spike!'

Each question I ask leads to a laugh,
Like walking in circles on a math path.
I tried to count the stars last night,
But fell asleep before the first light!

In search of answers, I found my phone,
It buzzed and chimed—a mind of its own!
So I Googled life, but saw just memes,
Confirming my age-old, silly dreams.

And as I wander with wit and cheer,
I know deep down there's nothing to fear.
For every riddle I think I found,
Just leads to giggles on this merry ground.

Breaths Between the Questions

I ponder deep with a bowl of stew,
As I ask my dog what to do.
He wags his tail and steals my bite,
'The secret to life, it's all about night!'

In moments of thought, I floss my brain,
Like trying to comprehend a train.
My thoughts run wild like cows in a field,
I just hope they don't refuse to yield!

I tossed my doubts like old t-shirts,
Awaiting the wisdom that never flirts.
When life throws a curve, just hit a home run,
Or eat marshmallows—either's good fun!

The breaths I take in looking for clues,
Are often filled with comedy, too.
For in the silence between each thought,
Lies laughter's echo in wisdom caught.

The Embrace of the Unanswered

Woke up one day with questions galore,
Like why is there traffic at the store?
I asked a cat, she just licked her paw,
And stared at me like I broke a law!

While seeking the truths wrapped in disguise,
I often get lost—oh what a surprise!
I asked the moon if he had a plan,
He winked and blushed like a bashful man.

With each silly thought, I scribble it down,
Wearing life's puzzles like a worn-out crown.
Dance with confusion, it's not out of reach,
In the chaos of thought, there's much to teach!

So here's to the questions that don't get solved,
In their tangled mess, I feel involved.
With a chuckle and smile, I spin in delight,
For the unanswered sparks joy in the night!

Pilgrimage of the Perpetually Curious

Pack your bags for a curious spree,
With snacks and giggles, just you and me.
We'll travel the world with eyes wide open,
In search of humor and old bread, broken.

I met a man who claimed to be wise,
But he couldn't tell me where I left my fries!
With each step forward, I lost myself more,
In a quest for where I left my keys at the store.

Oh, the places I've been and odd sights I've seen,
Like visiting that park with a dancing machine.
Every turn leads to a silly affair,
In the pilgrimage where questions fill the air.

And though I might wander without a clue,
With laughter as fuel, I'll always push through.
For in every detour, there's joy to be found,
In the comedy of life, I'm forever spellbound.

Finding the Compass Within

I took a map, it led me here,
To a buffet of endless cheer.
Where I forgot my phone and keys,
But found some laughter, if you please.

My compass spun like a top in flight,
Pointing to snacks, oh what a sight!
Lost in thought, I trip on cake,
Realizing my path is what I make.

With friends who cling like peanut butter,
We navigate through all the clutter.
Our laughs are charts, our smiles the stars,
As we meander past the chocolate bars.

So here's to paths that twist and twine,
Each misstep turning out just fine.
I may not know where I'm going next,
But I'll enjoy the ride—my life's an adventure text.

Remembering to Forget

I met a thought beneath my bed,
It whispered secrets, then fled.
Trying to grasp it was quite the feat,
Like catching noodles—what a treat!

I pondered hard on what I'd learned,
But every answer unreturned.
So I flipped a coin to take a break,
And ended up with cake and flake.

With every memory tucked away,
I search for treasures that betray.
I forgot my keys, but found some tunes,
To sing along to lost afternoons.

Letting go feels like a dance,
Where I trip and laugh, take a chance.
In forgetting, I stumble on gold,
Stories to cherish, daring and bold.

Riddles of the Soul's Journey

I asked my heart, 'What's the plan?'
It replied with a quirky spam.
'Take the left turn at the pie shop,
Then you'll find what makes you hop!'

Each riddle leaves me scratching heads,
While dodging fate, and cotton threads.
I laughed so hard at my own plight,
When paths turned into a bowling night.

I searched for wisdom in a sock,
Found a treasure map, what a shock!
With every step, I drew a line,
Connecting use with silly signs.

So in this dance of twist and curl,
I ponder not; I twirl and swirl.
If life's a riddle, I'm a fool,
Embracing chaos as my rule.

Canvases of the Unfinished

Behold my canvas, splashed with glee,
With colors bright, and yet quite free.
I started painting all my dreams,
But lost the brush; now paint's in streams.

Each stroke a story left to fate,
Some wild, some sad, some just too late.
It's abstract art, or so I say,
A masterpiece gone slightly gray.

Oh, the filters broke; what a sight!
A rainbow turned to black and white.
Yet here I stand with a cheeky grin,
Admiring chaos where it's been.

So here's to jobs half-done and free,
To laughter's brush and whimsy spree.
In every error lies my new start,
Each canvas tells a funny heart.

Navigating the Unknown

Lost in a maze of thoughts so bright,
I trip on my shoelaces, oh what a sight!
A compass points south, but I want to go north,
Guess I'll just wing it, for all it's worth.

The map's upside down, my snacks gone stale,
I thought I packed wisdom, but it's just kale.
With each step I take, a new question knocks,
Is it too late to ask for a shoelace box?

I met a wise turtle who said, "Take your time,"
While I scribble aims in silly rhyme.
He looks at me puzzled, then retreats to his shell,
Maybe this journey's not meant to end well.

So here I wander with coffee in hand,
Chasing rainbows, a flaky plan.
In this grand play of haphazard ways,
I'll wear pajamas during my quest haze.

A Journey Through the Unseen

Through the fog where the odd socks dwell,
I search for a hint, a secret to tell.
But they giggle and whisper, evading my gaze,
I'm starting to think it's a sock puppet phase.

The bushes are rustling, could it be fate?
Or just a raccoon sneaking off with my plate?
"Excuse me, good sir!" I shout in surprise,
But the raccoon just scurries, with glint in his eyes.

At the edge of the woods, a sign made of cheese,
It's not what I thought, but I'm brought to my knees.
In a world made of flavors, I ponder, I muse,
Are questions the answer, or merely a ruse?

So onward I travel, embracing the wild,
With visions of grandeur, like an overhyped child.
In the land of the unseen, I dance with delight,
And laugh at the shadows that give me a fright.

The Pursuit of Unwritten Stories

With a pen in my pocket and ink on my shoes,
I chase after stories, but nothing ensues.
They hide in the clouds, play tricks with my mind,
As I scribble on napkins, each word misaligned.

I met a wise fish who spoke in puns,
"Life's better with bubbles and lots of fun runs."
But between spoonerisms and jellyfish dreams,
I wander in circles, or so it seems.

Each page that I turn feels just like a prank,
As ideas jump out as I sit on a plank.
The ink spills like laughter in chaotic arrays,
Are unwritten tales worth the caffeine delays?

Yet, here's the kicker, beneath this chaos!
These stories, my friend, are the true boss.
With every wild laugh and scribbled mistake,
I find that the journey's the tale I must make.

Treading Water in Empty Spaces

Floating through air as though I can swim,
In pools of confusion, my chances seem grim.
I splash like a dolphin, flail like a whale,
Yet I find calm in chaos, such an odd tale.

The clock ticks loudly while I hold my breath,
Looking for answers in a game of chess.
"Checkmate!" says life, while I giggle in glee,
Skipping my turn, just to let my mind flee.

The walls are quite bland, but my thoughts are a riot,
In a theater of silence, oh how I try it!
What's next on the agenda? A dance with a chair?
Or a tea party hosted by a bear in despair?

So I tread in the stillness, no rush in my beat,
Creating a splash with whimsical feet.
In this empty expanse, humor lights the way,
And I'll keep floating until the end of my day.

Contours of an Incomplete Picture

My brush is missing half the hues,
A masterpiece of sneezes and muse.
The cat's my art critic, with fur so grand,
As I paint my life in a wobbly hand.

Each stroke whispers secrets unplanned,
Like dance moves lost in a quirky band.
I swear the canvas giggles and teases,
While my palette just sneezes and wheezes.

I dabble in chaos, a bit of flair,
Sprinkling doubt like confetti in air.
Yet in this jest, something feels right,
As laughter colors the shift of night.

In the end, it's a carnival show,
With colors that blend and boldly glow.
Through smears and chuckles, I'll find my way,
Creating a world where limelight will stay.

Silence Between the Notes

A kazoo plays in a symphony,
While my thoughts dance in sheer cacophony.
I tickle the ivories, hit all the wrong keys,
And the audience laughs while sipping their teas.

All the silence between every note,
Makes melodies jump like a bouncy boat.
I hum off-key, but fun's all around,
Even my dog nods to the goofy sound.

My music's a puzzle, each piece out of jam,
The rhythm's a workout for any old ham.
Yet who needs precision when joy is at stake,
We'll shake what we've got, for laughter's sweet sake.

So let's brew some noise, let's shake up this place,
With raucous tunes and an untamed grace.
In the play of our lives, every goof is a spark,
As we jazz up the night and giggle in the dark.

The Light of Unfinished Lanterns

I crafted a lantern with holes like cheese,
It flickers and wobbles but offers some tease.
With candles mismatched, it winks in delight,
As shadows throw parties each whimsical night.

The glow is uncertain, yet full of surprise,
While fireflies chuckle, flutter, and rise.
Every corner I light is a riddle, a game,
For who needs perfection when fun's in the flame?

I chase little whims like a kid with a kite,
As beams of my lantern create silly sights.
It's a dance of the light with a dash of the dark,
Where each flicker invites an improv of spark.

So here in my garden, with lights gone astray,
I'll shine with the laughter that comes out to play.
Unfinished and bright, I welcome the chance,
To twirl with my lantern in a whimsical dance.

Fables of the Unseen Journey

I set out on quests wearing mismatched socks,
Plot twists abound like cartoonish flocks.
With maps full of coffee spills, I embrace,
A landslide of giggles, a dizzying race.

Each step an adventure, a giggle to pen,
My navigational skills belong in a den.
Yet lo! The unseen brings laughter to roam,
As I trip over wisdom, misplacing my home.

A tale that unfolds in unexpected ways,
Where squirrels offer counsel in nutty displays.
With giggles as guides through the laughter and strife,
Every blunder becomes the spice of my life.

So here's to the travels and stories untold,
With humor my treasure, and joy my gold.
In fables of folly, I'll proudly chart,
The comedy written in the beat of my heart.

The Flicker of Forgotten Dreams

Once I dreamed of flying high,
But tripped on clouds, oh my, oh my!
The birds just laughed, a joyful sound,
As I fell back, feet on the ground.

In my mind, a chocolate tree,
Where rivers flow with lemonade, whee!
But I woke up, what a shame,
To find it was just a quirky game.

A quest for laughs in the moonlight,
Chasing shadows, feels so right,
But the floor's a trampoline, dear,
Bouncing back with silly cheer.

With each stumble, I still strive,
For the giggles that make me thrive,
In the maze of my silly schemes,
I'll find the flicker of lost dreams.

Mosaics of Hope and Struggle

Building hopes with mismatched bricks,
Dancing round with all my quirks,
Each piece tells a story grand,
Of dreams skewed by my own hand.

A puzzle missing half its face,
Yet here I am, a smile in place,
Crafting laughs from every crack,
In this mosaic, I'll not look back.

The cat that sings out tune so sweet,
While I juggle with two left feet,
Falling down, I take a chance,
To laugh aloud and join the dance.

So here's to life, the awkward jest,
With messy colors, I feel blessed,
In every stumble, joy does bloom,
Creating light from all the gloom.

The Pulse of an Unwritten Story

In the margins of my day,
Where butterflies decide to play,
I scribble thoughts in colors bright,
An unwritten tale takes flight.

With every tick of the clock's hand,
I'm plotting twists, oh isn't it grand?
Yet, coffee spills bring chaos neat,
As stories swirl beneath my feet.

A penguin on a skateboard zooms,
While I dodge all imaginary glooms,
With laughter echoing through the air,
I find my rhythm, without a care.

So let the pages dance and spin,
In this odd tale, I'll always win,
With laughter as my faithful guide,
This unwritten pulse will not subside.

In Search of the Unseen Fountain

I wander through a forest rare,
In search of laughter hiding there,
With each twist and turn I make,
I find more giggles with each shake.

The squirrels scheme a grand parade,
As I sit back, a charade made,
Their acorn hats, a sight to see,
Who knew joy could grow on trees?

A fountain bubbling, oh, what bliss,
I leap and splash with every kiss,
But it's soda pop, not water clear,
Still quenched by bubbly, fizzy cheer.

So here I trudge with wobbly grace,
In every stumble, I see a face,
The unseen fountain, laughter's cheer,
A treasure found, so crystal clear.

Fleeting Shadows of Purpose

In a café of forgotten dreams,
We sip on cups of milk and screams.
With cookies crumbling, thoughts take flight,
What's really wrong? Is it day or night?

We chase the silly, the bizarre and daft,
Hunting for treasures in a cereal raft.
The universe winks, a playful jest,
Tying our shoelaces? What a quest!

With jesters dancing on the edge of reason,
We ponder life like it's a changing season.
Searching for purpose in a sock drawer slide,
Maybe it's just where our mismatches hide!

So raise your glass to the silly pursuits,
As we dance with humor in floppy boots.
Embrace the chaos, don't fear the spree,
For in the laughter, we find the key!

Journey through the Unsung Realms

Wandering through lands where the oddballs meet,
We ask, 'What's next?' while lost in the street.
With compasses broken and maps upside-down,
A search for sense in this quaint little town.

Socks on our hands and shoes on our heads,
We march to the rhythms of unspoken threads.
The park bench philosopher offers a grin,
'The key's in the chocolate! Now let's begin!'

With hotdogs in hand, we contemplate fate,
Do we need a crystal ball or a plate?
In the tangle of giggles, the jokes intertwine,
Finding our purpose, one punchline at a time.

So sing with the squirrels and dance with the bees,
Life's a buffet of sarcastic cheese.
In this journey of laughter, we stroll hand-in-hand,
Exploring the realms of the humor-filled land!

Echoes of a Hidden Compass

In the attic of dreams where the lost socks dwell,
We ponder our wishes and wish them well.
The echoes of laughter bounce off the walls,
As we emulate penguins and imitate fowl.

With maps made of cookie dough and candy canes,
We navigate life through whimsical lanes.
The compass spins wildly, it points to the moon,
'Time for a dance in the light of a June!'

Draped in the chaos of mismatched reality,
We juggle our worries with pure vitality.
The world's a stage, and we've lost our cue,
'The secret!' we shout, 'Is to just be you!'

So let's skip down the road of the strange and surreal,
With echoes of laughter that joyfully reel.
A purpose feels close, like a pizza at noon,
With toppings of nonsense and a sprinkle of tune!

Whispers of the Uncharted Path

On the edge of the world, where the weirdos thrive,
We stumble through puzzles, feeling alive.
With donuts as maps and giggles as guides,
We're dressed in the quirks that the universe provides.

In the library of laughter, we flip through the shelves,
Finding hidden gems where the chaos dwells.
The whispers of wisdom drift in the air,
'There's always room for a banana split flair!'

With each quirky twist, we learn and we play,
Life's not just a game; it's a cabaret!
The spotlight's for those who dare to be bright,
In the uncharted world, laughter takes flight.

So toss all your questions—let's dance on the roof,
Embracing the madness, we'll find our own truth.
In the whispers of whimsy, we finally can see,
That humor's the compass; it's always been free!

In Search of Silent Conversations

I sit alone with a cup of tea,
Imagining chats with fish and bees.
They nod and blink, what do they say?
Guess I'll just sip and drift away.

A squirrel passes with quite the grin,
Could it be? A secret kin!
We share a laugh, it feels so right,
But then it darts off, out of sight.

In this café of make-believe,
I serve up thoughts, hope they receive.
The barista winks, as if in on,
The game I play from dusk till dawn.

So here I am, an artist proud,
Painting silence in a joyful crowd.
With each sip and giggle, absurdly grand,
I craft the meaning, cup in hand.

The Tapestry of Half-Formed Dreams

They say my dreams are quite a sight,
Woven with giggles, oh what a fright!
A unicorn wearing polka-dot shoes,
Strutting around with nothing to lose!

I chase a thought, it's fuzzy and round,
Like a lost balloon that can't be found.
It flits and flutters, a whimsical tease,
Making me giggle, oh how it frees!

These half-formed thoughts, an art of their own,
Dance through the chaos, like seeds, they're sown.
In napkin sketches or scribbles in space,
Who knew that nonsense could feel like grace?

Early mornings with coffee in tow,
Creating the world, just one silly show.
For in these dreams, so oddly streamed,
I find the laughter, or so it seemed.

Harvesting Echoes of the Past

I'm digging for treasures, in yesterday's soil,
What's this? A shoe? I'll give it a foil!
An umbrella with holes, a map with no route,
Maybe these echoes could bear me a doubt?

Old photos of pets, with a strange little grin,
A cat in a hat, that could never win.
I crop out the faces, just fill in the fun,
Just me and the laughter, oh, isn't it fun?

I gather old stories, like crops in the field,
Tales that are silly, but never concealed.
A ghost in the attic, was that really there?
Or just a figment born from thin air?

So here I am, collecting the past,
In a basket of chuckles, forever to last.
The echoes still giggle, with every new day,
Harvesting memories, in my own playful way.

Moments Lost to the Wind

A whisper of laughter, the breeze takes it far,
Floating through skies, like a lost shooting star.
I wave to the wind as it tickles my nose,
Fleeting like dreams, where the silliness grows.

Chasing small moments, like bubbles in air,
They pop with a giggle, and vanish, I swear.
A dance with the shadows, a skip and a twirl,
In this silly game, see the world start to whirl.

Oh, what fun to chase after fluff,
Collecting the giggles and all things absurd.
Each moment a treasure, each chuckle a gem,
Lost to the wind, but happy to stem.

For laughter is magic, that we can retrieve,
Despite moments wandering, I firmly believe.
That joy is the point, in this whimsical spin,
Even when moments are lost to the wind.

Searching for Stars in the Gloom

In the depths of night, I search for light,
With a flashlight that flickers, my vision takes flight.
I peer through the fog, my eyes open wide,
Stumbling on shadows, oh what a ride!

The stars play hide and seek, quite a fun game,
But tripping on rocks, well, who am I to blame?
I moonwalk with wonder, like I'm Michael Jackson,
While wondering why my friend took the wrong direction.

A comet zooms past, but it's just a car's beam,
I laugh as I chase after a wild, sleeping dream.
Each twinkle a chuckle, each wink a cheer,
Who knew that seeking stars would be funny here?

In this cosmic dance, I'm just playing along,
With jokes about gravity—oh, how they throng!
So here's to the nights full of quirky delight,
As I fumble through shadows, searching for bright!

A Tapestry of Lost Dreams

A woven mishmash of hopes that once soared,
Now tangled and jumbled, I can't be ignored.
I had dreams of grandeur, like flying a kite,
   But ended up in a tangle, what a sight!

I thought I'd be famous, a rock star with flair,
But my only audience is my cat in despair.
He yawns through my ballads, then falls back to sleep,
While I strum my heart out, for my passion runs deep.

My plans are like socks that vanish from sight,
One goes to the laundry, the other takes flight.
I chase after fabric, and find it absurd,
   That my dreams are unravelling, just like a bird!

With threads of ambition, I sew up the seams,
My comedic missteps, they become my great themes.
So let's toast to the chaos, the laughter, the schemes,
In this tapestry of lost dreams, I'll regain my gleam!

In Pursuit of the Elusive Light

I chase after beams that flicker and sway,
Like a moth to a bulb, come night or day.
Every time I think I've found the right glow,
It's just the fridge humming—don't you love the show?

Running in circles, I slip on the floor,
My light at the end? Just the exit door.
I ask a wise owl, he just hoots with glee,
While I ponder my purpose by the old oak tree.

A lantern in hand, I light up my path,
But trip on a root, oh, what a good laugh!
The darkness around me seems in on the joke,
As I dance like a fool, surrounded by smoke.

Each spark is a giggle, each shadow a cheer,
Illuminating moments so vibrant, so near.
In pursuit of the light, I find it's not bright,
But it sure makes for stories worth telling tonight!

Fragments of Thoughts Unraveled

My mind is a puzzle, with pieces all gone,
I search for that corner, but it feels like a con.
I had a bright idea, or so it is said,
But it vanished like socks when you've just made your bed.

I scribble on napkins with crayons galore,
Each doodle a question—what was that for?
I try to connect dots, but they dance out of line,
Leaving me laughing with coffee and twine.

Once upon a thought, I wrote in a haze,
Now it's just squiggles—my thoughts in a maze.
Each fragment I gather, a jigsaw of quips,
With nothing but giggles escaping my lips.

So here's to the banter, the silly and free,
Embracing confusion like it's meant to be.
With thoughts that unravel, I chuckle and sigh,
In this carnival of whims, I'm just passing by!

Beyond the Horizon of Tomorrow

In the land where socks go to hide,
I tripped on my thoughts, took a slide.
With a map made of marshmallows and dreams,
I searched for sense in chocolate streams.

With a compass that spins in a whirl,
I asked a goldfish, 'What makes you twirl?'
It bubbled and swam, then swam away,
I jotted it down—maybe it's play?

Inspired by clouds shaped like rhinos,
I danced through the meadows of big buffalo.
With each silly step, I laughed with glee,
Chasing the echoes of my lost keys.

As stars threw confetti upon my head,
I wondered, is this the place for bread?
But who needs a sandwich when you can fly,
With laughter as wings, oh me, oh my!

Chasing the Flicker of Purpose

With a tiny flashlight and fuzzy old map,
I waded through puddles and avoided the flap.
I asked the moon, 'Do you think I'm cool?'
It winked and said, 'Only when you drool.'

Tickling the time, I giggled and spun,
Following fireflies, they said life's fun!
They flickered like candles in a cake,
I searched for meaning in each slice I bake.

A squirrel with glasses joined on the side,
He said, 'Just relax, take a wild ride!'
With each twirl and skip, we lost track of the clock,
While figuring out why time loves to mock.

We built a castle made of sticky notes,
With dreams written down in funny little quotes.
The humor we found was the greatest surprise,
In laughter and chaos, purpose can rise!

A Dance with Ambivalence

In a waltz with confusion, I stepped on my toes,
My partner was doubt, in mismatched clothes.
We twirled through the halls of what might have been,
Mumbling sweet nothings and secretly grinned.

Every tango was filled with a riddle,
My brain played the kazoo and suddenly whittled.
I pondered aloud, 'What's the deal with this cheer?'
The curtain just laughed, then disappeared.

A cha-cha with choices, I hustled with flair,
But ended up pirouetting into a chair.
With hiccups and giggles, we spun round the room,
As confetti of questions started to bloom.

In the midst of this dance, I found some delight,
In the quirks of indecision, I twirled with the night.
With every misstep, I came to embrace,
That laughter through chaos was my saving grace!

Sifting Through the Sands of Time

With a shovel and bucket, I dug through the days,
Uncovering treasures in curious ways.
I found an old shoe and a spoon made of gold,
Tales of adventures that never get old.

Sifting through whispers, I chuckled aloud,
At memories zigzagging, under a cloud.
A crab pointed sideways, said, 'What's the rush?'
I paused for a selfie, then came out of the crush.

Grains of giggles and sandcastles tall,
Each grain held a memory, each little squall.
I cartwheeled with time like a cat with a hat,
While searching for meaning in chatty old rats.

With a wink and a nod, I let out a cheer,
For each silly moment that brought me right here.
As the tide rolled in, embracing the jest,
I found in the chaos, I felt truly blessed!

Serpentine Paths of Discovery

I took a turn, then slipped on gum,
My shoes are shoes, but feel like dumb.
I chase a thought, it runs away,
Like my cat on a busy day.

I crossed a road, the chicken's there,
It chewed my thoughts, I swear, I swear!
A sign above, it points and grins,
I lost my way, but found some sins.

The twisty trails like maze in fun,
Each step I take, there's more to shun.
With every twist and every bend,
I laugh aloud at where I tend.

In shadows deep, I dance with fate,
A silly fate that can't relate.
Yet still I wander, without a map,
A joyful jig, a silly flap.

Cracked Mirrors of Reflection

I peeked into a glass so spry,
It showed my face and made me sigh.
My hair's a mess, a total wreck,
Looks like I lost a game of check!

The mirror laughed, it gave a wink,
"You're way more fun than you might think!"
With every crack, a story told,
Of dreams and schemes that never rolled.

I tried to shine, but tripped and fell,
The shards of glass, they rang a bell.
"Who's that?" I asked, "And where's the proof?"
The answer danced just 'neath the roof.

In jigsaw pieces, I'm a spree,
A patchwork quilt of glee and glee.
So here's to me and all my flaws,
Let's raise a glass, and clap our paws!

Assembling the Pieces of Now

I found a puzzle piece of cheese,
It made me giggle, started to tease.
"Where's the corner?" I lost my grip,
A slice of life, a buttered trip.

In time's big box, I sift for clues,
Some bits are gray, and some are blues.
A shoe, a hat, a rubber duck,
I swear this chaos is sheer luck!

Each piece I found, it gives a nudge,
With every fit, I start to judge.
But who needs order or a grand scheme?
Life's just a wild, whimsical dream.

So here I sit, a child's delight,
Building my wonder with all my might.
If pieces don't fit, that's quite alright,
Let's dance around in silly light!

The Clarity Within the Fog

I squint through haze, a gassy cloud,
Where facts and fables meet the crowd.
A foghorn blows, or was that me?
I'm lost, yet found, just wait and see.

The trees look like they wear a coat,
A fuzzy cloak, or maybe a boat.
"Hello!" I shout, "Is someone there?"
But echoes mock; I just despair.

With every step, the fog renowned,
It gets a laugh, it spins around.
So I embrace my bumbling stroll,
A waltz in fog—what a wild goal!

Through cloudy scenes, I sway and swing,
Finding joy in the nonsense spring.
In misty moments, I see the cheer,
Clarity comes, but never here!

Foraging for Hints of Clarity

In the cupboard of thoughts, I rummage around,
Finding crumbs of wisdom scattered on the ground.
A recipe for happiness, just a pinch of glee,
But I can't find the salt—oh, where can it be?

Poke the fridge for answers, there's nothing but cheese,
Maybe some pickles could help set me at ease.
Yet here in the chaos, I mix up my spells,
Sipping on dreams from glittering wells.

With a jar of old jelly and a dash of doubt,
I sprinkle my queries, therein, I shout:
'Is it love or lasagna that fills up my plate?'
As laughter emerges, let's not contemplate.

A basket of giggles becomes my delight,
While hunting for clarity, I dance through the night.
In this kitchen of life, I can finally see,
That sometimes the mess is the key to be free!

The Color of Untold Realities

In a world painted gray, I seek the bright hues,
A splash of ridiculousness in everyday views.
I trip over wisdom that's mixed up with paint,
My thoughts runneth over like a mad little saint.

The sky wore a frown, while the sun turned to tease,
Clouds bickered and giggled, like swarming bees.
A rainbow of laughter swept down from above,
Perhaps the key to this chaos is love.

I gaze at my shoes, they're a curious sight,
With one blue, one green—oh what a delight!
Like mismatched socks, life jesters and jives,
In colors of nutty, absurdity thrives.

So let's swirl the colors, let's dip our toes,
In a canvas of chaos, where whimsy still grows.
In the festival of life, let's dance and create,
For the laughter we find shows it's never too late.

Beneath the Surface of the Everyday

Underneath the routine, a circus could thrive,
With jugglers of chaos and clowns full of jive.
I watch as the toaster performs its great feat,
Burning my toast, yet still brings me a treat.

Waking up early, I swear it's a sin,
My coffee cup's empty, let the madness begin.
The stairs start to sing as I tumble with grace,
Each step is a riddle; it's quite the embrace.

Fruits in the bowl have lost their ambition,
They chat about politics—what a rendition!
But my bananas are wise, and they all know my name,
In this ballet of breakfast, we all play the game.

So here's to the mundane, the daily charades,
To finding the funny in life's silly trades.
For the joy isn't hidden; it shimmers and glows,
Beneath every moment, a laughter that flows.

Navigating Through Quiet Chaos

There's a storm in the teacup, a dance in the mug,
While the cat wears a crown—oh, what an odd bug!
The kettle whistling jokes, bubbles burst into views,
As I sail through this tempest in my plastic shoes.

The laundry's a mountain, the dishes a sea,
Yet somehow I'm sailing, just sipping my tea.
With socks as my sails, I let the wind steer,
And laughter becomes my compass, so clear.

Navigating dishes that pile in high stacks,
With a map of giggles and a ship full of snacks.
Caught in the currents of chores drifting by,
I wave at the chaos, with a wink and a sigh.

So I keep on this journey in a world full of zest,
Finding humor in mishaps, I'm simply the best.
For amidst all the chaos, let fun take the lead,
In this grand little voyage, there's joy to be freed!

www.ingramcontent.com/pod-product-compliance
Lightning Source LLC
Chambersburg PA
CBHW071846160426
43209CB00003B/436